FIRE PROOF—NOT DEATH PROOF CONSTRUCTION

BOSTON HERALD

6789

Cornerstones of Freedom

The Story of
THE TRIANGLE FACTORY FIRE

By Zachary Kent

CP CHILDRENS PRESS®

CHICAGO

Victims of the Triangle fire

Library of Congress Cataloging-in-Publication Data

Kent, Zachary.

  The story of the Triangle factory fire.
  (Cornerstones of freedom)
  Includes index.
  Summary: Describes the 1911 fire at the Triangle
Shirtwaist factory in New York, the conditions surround-
ing the disaster, and its effect on industrial safety
after the event.
  1. Triangle Shirtwaist Company — Fire, 1911 —
Juvenile literature. 2. Clothing factories — New York
(N.Y.) — Safety measures — History — 20th century — Juvenile
literature. 3. Industrial safety — New York (N.Y.) —
History — 20th century — Juvenile literature. 4. New York
(N.Y.) — Industries — History — 20th century — Juvenile
literature. [1. Triangle Shirtwaist Company — Fire,
1911. 2. Industrial safety — History.] I. Title.
II. Series.
F128.5.K34 1989   363.3′79   88-36223
ISBN 0-516-04742-6

A muffled blast brought people running along the New York City streets on the afternoon of March 25, 1911. The sudden noise sounded "like a big puff," exclaimed one witness, followed by the crashing of glass. At the corner of Washington Place and Greene Street curious men and women gazed up at the Asch Building. The ten-story structure contained clothing factories and related businesses. Now from the street, observers could see black smoke drifting from some upper windows. "Within another minute," described bystander James Cooper, "the entire eighth floor was spouting little jets of flame."

Soon Cooper saw something that looked "like a bale of dark dress goods" dropping out of a window. "Someone's in there all right," declared a bystander. "He's trying to save the best cloth."

Then a second bundle of cloth fell. As it tumbled toward the ground, the wind tore at the bundle. Suddenly the onlookers gasped in horror. The wind, Cooper recalled, "disclosed the form of a girl shooting down to instant death."

From the windows of the Triangle Shirtwaist Company roaring flames licked out. The workers inside were trapped by the fire that blazed around them. Hopelessly the workers climbed out onto the ledges or jumped from windows. Bells clanged and whistles shrieked, as horses galloped into the street pulling fire engines. "Don't jump! Here they come!" shouted frantic bystanders. Their hair and clothes on fire, still the workers jumped. "The first thing I saw," declared fireman Frank Rubino, "was a man's body come crashing down through . . . a sidewalk shed. . . . We kept going. We turned into Greene Street and began to stretch our hoses. The bodies were hitting all around us."

Unable to reach them, shocked bystanders watched helplessly as workers jumped.

The fire killed 146 workers within twenty minutes.

The bodies, burned black and broken by their falls, smashed together in heaps. United Press reporter William Shepherd exclaimed, "The floods of water from the firemen's hoses that ran into the gutter were actually red with blood." Within twenty minutes the last body dropped from the flaming Triangle factory window ledge. Altogether the tragedy claimed the lives of 146 innocent workers. In the days that followed, outraged Americans demanded to know how such a horrible thing could happen.

"My building is fireproof," insisted Joseph J. Asch, the owner of the Asch Building. In fact, according to 1911 New York City fire codes, the ten-year-old building had been safe enough. Two

emergency staircases led down to the street with exits on every floor. Also a winding metal fire escape hung bolted on the wall of the inner courtyard. Filled water buckets could be found on every floor and rolled fire hoses, suspended on the stairwell walls, connected with the roof's water tank. It hardly mattered that there was no water sprinkler system in the ceilings, and few people seemed to care that workers were never given fire drills. Not even fire escapes were required by the law. It would take a terrible fire to reveal the Asch Building's hidden dangers.

Joseph Asch leased the top three floors of his building to the Triangle Shirtwaist Company. Max Blanck and Isaac Harris, the successful owners of this large factory, made shirtwaists, ladies' close-fitting blouses very popular at that time. Even on Saturday, March 25, 1911, the Triangle factory was busy. In the tenth floor business and shipping offices, accountants added sales figures in ledgers, and packers filled boxes with finished orders. On the eighth and ninth floors 500 workers created thousands of shirtwaists. Each floor measured roughly 100 feet by 100 feet and was crowded with long wooden tables. Dozens of cutters sliced sleeves and other shirt patterns from layers of fabric. Seated

Crowded working conditions were commonplace.

The Triangle factory may have looked like this unidentified factory.

closely side by side, rows of young women bent over whirring sewing machines stitching the blouse sections together. Most of these hard workers were Italian and Russian Jewish girls just arrived in America and glad to have their jobs. In addition, machinists scurried about, oiling machines, and replacing broken belts and sewing needles.

Cloth was piled everywhere. Great rolls of silk, lace, and muslin jammed wallshelves, ready to be used. Wicker baskets blocked the aisles, heaped full of finished shirtwaists. On the cutting tables long stretches of material 180 layers thick waited to be sliced. Beneath these tables, in great bins, the cutters tossed useless cloth scraps. Every two months a rag man hauled away more than 2,000 pounds of fabric cuttings from the Triangle factory.

At about 4:30 P.M. that Saturday the eighth floor quitting bell rang. The humming of the sewing machines stopped, and chairs scraped on the wooden floor. Clutching their weekly pay envelopes the sewing machine operators walked down the narrow aisles. Chatting and laughing, they edged toward the dressing room to get their coats.

Hundreds of workers were crowded together.

Suddenly Eva Harris, the sister of owner Isaac Harris, smelled something burning. "I looked to the cutting tables," she later exclaimed. "At the second table, through the slot under the top, I saw the red flames." No one ever learned exactly how the fire started, but the cutters often smoked cigarettes. "A cutter let a match fall . . ." one survivor afterwards insisted. Triangle production manager Samuel Bernstein heard Eva Harris yell—he turned and saw the blaze. "It was in a rag bin," he later declared, "and it jumped right up."

Cutters grabbed water pails and splashed the flames. But still the blaze rose from beneath the table. "Fire!" people shouted. Choking smoke began to fill the air and flames reached up toward the ceiling. Manager Bernstein threw more water and shouted orders. Shipping clerk Louis Senderman rushed into the stairwell and dragged in a water hose. Someone yanked at the water valve, but it was rusted solid and the hose was rotted through in places. Suddenly a draft from an open elevator door sent flaming scraps of cloth floating through the room. A young assistant machinist screamed and pulled on Bernstein's hand. "I turned around and looked at him and the boy was burning. He ran away from me into the smoke."

Already the fire raged out of control. In horror Bernstein yelled to a machinist, "Try to get the girls out!" Through the whirling smoke and flames 225 men and women fought to escape. The fire blocked the Greene Street exit. Forcing open the Washington Street door, dozens of terrified women pushed and clawed their way down the 33-inch-wide stairway. Crushed against the elevator doors Irene Seivos remembered, "I broke the window. . .with my hands and screamed, 'Fire! Fire! Fire!' It was so hot we could scarcely breathe."

About a dozen workers remembered the fire escape. Struggling out the window they tripped down the twisting iron steps. A few raced to the bottom and dropped the last feet into the courtyard. Others climbed through the window onto the sixth floor where they huddled until a policeman arrived and broke the locked stairway door open for them.

At the outbreak of the blaze, eighth floor bookkeeper Dinah Lifschitz telephoned upstairs to the tenth floor office: "There is a fire!" Soon smoke drifted up the stairways and in the windows. Dazed and frightened secretaries and shipping clerks ran to the passenger elevators. "Save us! Save us!" the young women screamed, shoving forward. In the middle of the smoky office, stunned owner Max Blanck clutched his two small daughters who were visiting that day. "To the roof! To the roof!" he heard his partner Isaac Harris shouting. "Girls, let us go to the roof!" Through the black haze the workers scurried up the Greene Street staircase. Halfway up, the rising flames already leapt in a stairway window. Triangle workers staggered onto the roof with scorched clothing and smoldering hair.

Clouds of smoke and tongues of flames licked over the edges of the roof. On the Greene Street side, the adjoining building stood ten feet taller than the Asch Building. Endangered workers boosted each other to safety, until the heat and flames there became too great. On the Washington Place side, a New York University building towered fifteen feet above the Asch Building. Alerted by fire engine sirens, billowing smoke, and shrieking voices, young men in Professor Frank Sommer's tenth floor law class ran to their roof. With painters' ladders, the students bridged the gap to the Asch Building. Forming a rescue line they heroically helped many frightened Triangle employees escape the approaching flames.

Meanwhile 250 workers were trapped on the ninth floor of the Triangle factory. "We didn't have a chance," recalled Rose Glantz. "The people on the eighth floor must have seen the fire start and grow. The people on the tenth floor got the warning over the telephone. But with us on the ninth, all of a sudden the fire was all around. The flames were coming in through many of the windows." Workers panicked and screamed as the flames set rag bins and wicker baskets ablaze around them. Shouts of

"Fire!" sent many workers rushing to the Greene Street exit.

"The girls behind us were screaming and crying," Tessa Benani declared. "Several of them, as the flames crept up closer, ran into the smoke, and we heard them scream as the flames caught their clothes. One little girl who worked at the machine opposite me cried out in Italian, 'Goodbye, goodbye!' I have not seen her since." Those who got through the narrow doorway ran the fiery gauntlet to the roof or down the stairs to Greene Street. However, a great barrel of sewing machine oil blocked part of the stairway. When the fire lit the barrel, its roaring explosion soon cut off the Greene Street exit.

On the Washington Place side, workers fought each other to get to the stairway exit there. The

Editorial cartoon shows how the locked stairway doors trapped some of the workers.

door was locked. Frantically they pounded the wood and screamed for help. Trapped people turned and ran in terror through the smoke and flames. Rose Cohen later exclaimed, "Girls were lying on the floor—fainted. People were stepping on them. Other girls were trying to climb over the machines. Some were running with their hair burning." "Surka, where are you, Surka?" cried out one man as he searched for his young sister. Dozen of girls staggered into the ninth floor dressing room. Coughing on the smoke, they clung together. Firemen later found fifty-eight girls burned to death there, their faces raised toward a little window.

The two passenger elevator operators, Gaspar Mortillalo and Joseph Zito, answered the shrieks and banging as quickly as they could. After trips to the eighth and tenth floors, they hurried their cars to the ninth. "When I first opened the elevator door on the ninth floor," Zito remembered, "all I could see was a crowd of girls and men with great flames and smoke right behind them." As many as thirty people shoved into cars designed to carry no more than fifteen. Again and again the emptied elevators made the frightening journey back from the lobby. Finally the right-hand elevator was unable to rise above the eighth floor's scorching flames. The heat had bent its track in the elevator shaft.

Then Joseph Zito's left-hand elevator refused to move upward. He heard crashing thumps on his roof. Young women were jumping down the open elevator shaft. "A body struck the top of the elevator and bent the iron," Zito exclaimed. "A minute later another one hit." A few lucky girls grabbed the elevator cable. The friction burned their hands as they slid down ninety feet. Most, however, plunged to their deaths.

Some workers trapped on the ninth floor broke through the shuttered windows to the fire escape. Panic-stricken they fought their way onto the winding metal stairs. Mary Bucelli honestly admitted, "I was throwing them out of the way. No matter whether they were in front of me or coming from in back of me, I was pushing them down. I was only looking out for my own life." In no time the intense heat and the weight of the fleeing workers bent and twisted the iron slats and railings.

Sixteen-year-old Abe Gordon, a Triangle button puncher, wisely ducked inside an open window on the sixth floor. "I still had one foot on the fire escape," he later exclaimed, "when I heard a loud noise and looked back up. The people were falling all around me. The fire escape was collapsing." Flung from the crumpled platforms and stairs, screaming people plummeted down to the courtyard. Some

This fire escape
collapsed under
the weight of the
fleeing workers.

When the fire escape collapsed, many victims fell to their deaths through the skylight (A). Two young girls were killed by the picket fence (C). Others fell into the courtyard (E). Twenty-five bodies were recovered from this area.

bodies smashed through a basement skylight. A few thudded against the iron courtyard fence. "As the fire-crazed victims were thrown..." reported the New York *Herald*, "several struck on the sharp-tipped palings. The body of one woman was found with several iron spikes driven entirely through it." Altogether less than twenty workers successfully escaped by using the flimsy fire escape.

On the Washington Place and Greene Street sidewalks shocked bystanders helplessly watched the drama at the ninth floor windows. Sheets of flame and blinding smoke forced dozens of workers to these openings. First one jumped and then another. Some girls inched along the ledge until the flames became unbearable. One stunned girl slowly opened her pocketbook and threw away a handful of money, her weekly pay. The bills glided in the air and the coins rang in the cobblestone street as she jumped. Another girl carefully balanced on the ledge with her hands on her hips. Suddenly she raised her hands and gestured at the stunned crowd before toppling forward.

Newsman William Shepherd witnessed the tragic spectacle. On the Washington Place side he noticed that the jumpers "tried to fall feet down. I watched one girl falling. She waved her arms, trying to keep her body upright until the very instant she struck the sidewalk."

One heart-rending scene especially shook the newsman. A young man deliberately helped three girls to the window sill and let them drop. Then he carefully assisted a fourth girl out the window. She seemed to be his sweetheart. "I saw her put her arms around him and kiss him," remembered Shepherd. "Then he held her into space—and dropped her. Quick as a flash, he was on the window sill himself. His coat fluttered upwards —the air filled his trouser legs as he came down....Together they went into eternity."

By Shepherd's count sixty-two Triangle employees jumped from the Asch Building's roof and

The fire
department's
seventy-foot
ladder could
only reach the
sixth floor.

windows. All the while, as the frightful minutes
ticked, companies of New York City firemen battled
the blaze and tried to save lives. "Raise the ladders!" shouted bystanders. Men of hook and ladder
company 20 hurriedly cranked up their tallest ladder. The crowd moaned when they saw that the
seventy-foot ladder could only reach the sixth floor.

Firemen opened life nets, and spectators joined in,
firmly holding their edges. Three bodies struck the
first net at the same time. Fire captain Howard
Ruch figured the falling force of each person
amounted to 11,000 pounds. "The bodies . . . carried
[the nets] to the sidewalk. The force was so great it

took the men off their feet; they turned somersaults over onto the bodies....The men's hands were bleeding, the nets were torn and some caught fire." "What good were life nets?" sadly commented Fire Chief Edward J. Worth.

Other firefighters grasped hoses as pump engines sent tons of water streaming into the burning building. Half an hour after the first alarm, the fire was under control. However, this relief came too late to save 146 Triangle workers. As wisps of smoke and steam rose from the drenched Asch Building, survivors staggered through the crowds with ripped clothes and smoke-smudged faces. Doctors treated burn victims and rushed them by ambulance to

Corner of the ninth floor after the fire was put out.

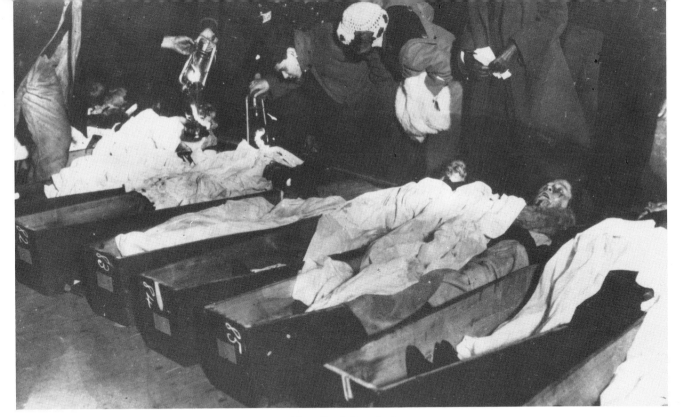
Relatives identify victims in the morgue.

hospitals. Others examined the bodies of the piled jumpers, hoping to find some evidence of life. Police lines held back the surging spectators. Anxious relatives of Triangle workers sobbed and prayed. The walls and floors of the "fireproof" building remained intact but fire wreckage lay everywhere.

By 6:20 Chief Edward F. Croker led a team of firemen up the stairs to the Triangle factory. Even then some of the window frames still burned. The hellish scene stunned Chief Croker. The New York *World* declared, "In the drifting smoke, he [saw] bodies burned to bare bones, skeletons bending over sewing machines." Firemen carried the bodies, wrapped in canvas, down the stairs or lowered them from the windows with ropes and pullies. Into the night sirens wailed as police wagons carried away the dead in coffins.

On a covered dock on the East River at Twenty-sixth Street police set up a temporary morgue. Inside, policemen, doctors, and nurses numbered the coffins, tried to identify the corpses, and recorded the personal possessions found on them. After midnight the pier gates swung open. "Come on! Come on! It's all ready now!" called out a policeman. Fearfully, crowds of waiting friends and relatives walked forward. Slowly they passed the rows of open coffins searching for missing loved ones. Suddenly a little woman wearing a shawl dropped to her knees and screamed. The first identification had been made at coffin number 15.

Policemen carry a coffin to the morgue.

"I am looking for my sister, Bettina," said young Joseph Miale as he searched among the coffins. One badly burned body wore a ring. When Miale saw it he staggered backward. "That is her ring," he exclaimed. During the next days thousands of people stepped through the ghastly morgue until only seven burned bodies remained unidentified and unclaimed.

The Triangle fire shocked the city. New Yorkers, rich and poor, swiftly donated money to help the families of victims. Altogether the Red Cross and other agencies offered $120,000 for relief. No amount of money, however, could replace the dead. Day after day horse-drawn hearses carried caskets off to city graveyards.

"Won't it ever be safe to earn our bread?" bitterly cried the mother of one fourteen-year-old victim. Many others also voiced anger over the causes of the tragedy, as public outrage swept through the city. On April 2, 1911, the Women's Trade Union League held a protest meeting at the Metropolitan Opera House.

"This is not the first time girls have been burned alive in the city," W.T.U.L. officer Rose Schneiderman forcefully reminded the audience. "Every week I must learn of the untimely death of one of my sister workers. Every year thousands of us are maimed. The life of men and women is so cheap and property is so sacred! There are so many of us for one job, it matters little if 140-odd are burned to death." Schneiderman and other speakers urged renewed union activity and strikes to force safer work conditions.

On April 5 Mayor William Gaynor ordered that the seven unknown Triangle victims be buried quietly in a city cemetery in Brooklyn. Working class New Yorkers chose that wet and rainy day to turn out and show their feelings. "The skies wept," reported the New York *World,* "as 80,000 working men and women marched in procession . . ." Past a watching crowd of 250,000 they moved along Fifth Avenue in the drenching downpour. Many of the working girls wore armbands reading, "We mourn our loss." Behind an empty hearse drawn by six

Memorial parade held for the workers.

white horses, survivors of the fire silently walked to the muffled beat of drums. Only when the marchers reached Washington Square Park, within view of the blackened Asch Building, did the mourners openly express their sadness. "It was one long-drawn-out, heart-piercing cry," declared the *World*, "the mingling of thousands of voices..."

In the days following the fire, city officials sifted through the charred rubble at the Asch Building and tried to fix the fault for the tragedy. Fire Chief Croker angrily stated, "There wasn't a fire escape anywhere fronting on the street by which these unfortunate girls could escape." Doors that opened inward instead of outward, overcrowding in work areas, and blocked exits also were to blame. Fire

Fireman inspects the charred ruins of the ninth floor.

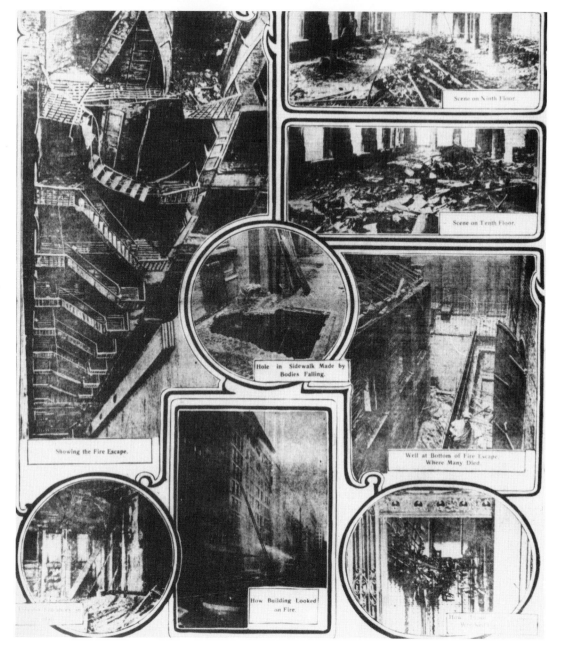

Page from the New York *Evening Journal* showing scenes from the Triangle fire.

Marshal William Beers stunned New Yorkers by soon declaring, "I can show you 150 loft buildings far worse than this one." Lillian D. Wald of the Joint Board of Sanitary Control also reported on the general situation. "The conditions as they now exist are hideous. . . .Our investigators have shown that there are hundreds of buildings which invite disaster just as much as did the Asch structure."

Accused of ignoring their employees' safety, Triangle owners Blanck and Harris were charged with manslaughter. During the three week trial angry citizens packed the courtroom. Outside, in the corridors, women screamed, "Murderers! Murderers! Make them suffer for killing our children!" Lawyers argued that Blanck and Harris kept all of the Triangle doors locked during the workday, therefore causing many of the deaths. Weighing the evidence, however, the jury returned a verdict of not guilty. "I cannot see that anyone was responsible for the disaster," explained juror H. Houston Hierst. "It seems to me to have been an act of the Almighty." The New York *Call* viewed the matter differently. "Capital can commit no crime," it angrily declared, "when it is in pursuit of profits."

Furious New Yorkers refused to let the issue rest. In October 1911 the city established a Bureau of Fire Prevention to inspect safety standards in other buildings. Five months earlier the New York State legislature created a special Factory Investigating Commission. Through the next four years Commission investigators crawled and pried through the rooms and cellars of factories and tenement houses

In 1961, the fiftieth anniversary of the Triangle Fire, a plaque was dedicated to the fire victims. From the left, Pauline Newman, former union organizer for International Ladies' Garment Workers' Union (ILGWU), Frances Perkins, who witnessed the fire and later served as secretary of labor, Rose Schneiderman, former president of the National Women's Trade Union League, David Dubinsky, former ILGWU organizer, and Ben Aaronson, former deputy assistant fire chief, New York all across the state. They examined workers' filthy living conditions and witnessed the dangers of crippling machinery and long work hours in dusty, dirty firetraps.

As a result of the Commission's shocking findings, New York State quickly passed thirty-three new labor laws by 1914. These laws formed the foundation of New York State's Industrial Code, the finest in the nation. Soon other states followed New York's example and enacted protective labor laws.

One Factory Commission investigator had witnessed the fateful Triangle fire. Frances Perkins said, "We heard the fire engines and rushed . . . to see what was going on. . . .We got there just as they started to jump. I shall never forget the frozen horror which came over us as we stood with our hands on our throats watching that horrible sight, knowing that there was no help."

In 1933 President Franklin Roosevelt named Frances Perkins secretary of labor. She and other social reformers dedicated their lives to insuring worker safety throughout the country. "They did not die in vain and we will never forget them," vowed Perkins. From the ashes of the tragic Triangle factory fire came help for millions of United States laborers today.

Workers in an unidentified sweatshop

About the Author

Zachary Kent grew up in Little Falls, New Jersey. He is a graduate of St. Law-
rence University and holds a teaching certificate in English. Following college he was
employed at a New York City literary agency for two years until he decided to launch
a career as a writer. To support himself while writing, he has worked as a taxi driver,
a shipping clerk, and a house painter.

Mr. Kent has had a lifelong interest in American history. As a boy the study of the
United States presidents was his special hobby. His collection of presidential items
includes books, pictures, and games, as well as several autographed letters.

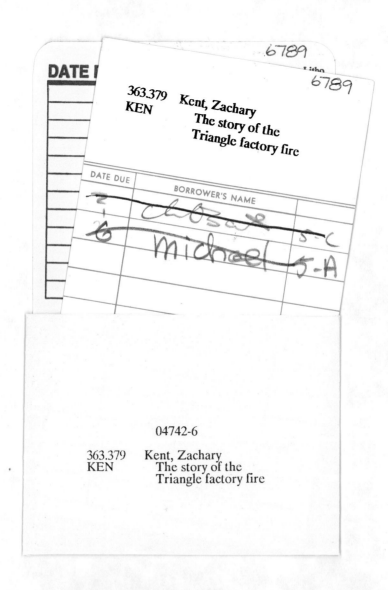